History of
J.M.W

A Biography

By Howard Brinkley

BookCaps™ Study Guides
www.bookcaps.com

© 2014. All Rights Reserved.

Table of Contents

ABOUT LIFECAPS 3
INTRODUCTION 4
CHAPTER 1: EARLY LIFE 6
CHAPTER 2: EDUCATION 10
CHAPTER 3: EARLY CAREER 18
CHAPTER 4: LATER LIFE AND CAREER 43
CHAPTER 5: JOSEPH MALLORD WILLIAM TURNER AND JOHN RUSKIN 50
CHAPTER 6: LAST WORKS 60
CHAPTER 7: DEATH AND LEGACY 70
BIBLIOGRAPHY 89

About LifeCaps

LifeCaps is an imprint of BookCaps™ Study Guides. With each book, a lesser known or sometimes forgotten life is recapped. We publish a wide array of topics (from baseball and music to literature and philosophy), so check our growing catalogue regularly (www.bookcaps.com) to see our newest books.

Introduction

In 2005, the British Broadcasting Corporation sponsored a program to find the greatest painting in Britain. Any painting hanging in a British art gallery was eligible to become The Greatest Painting in Britain, whether it was created by an Englishman or not. This was the first survey of its kind ever conducted, and was not a frivolous exercise for the organizers who explained the competition as a way to "tell us a great deal about how 21st Century, multicultural Britain sees itself."

After every work of art in the country was evaluated, a short list of finalists by British, Italian, Dutch, Belgian and French artists was announced. There were heavy hitters like *Still Life: Vase with Fifteen Sunflowers* by Vincent Van Gogh that had set a record for the most money ever paid for a work of art when it sold for $40 million in 1987 (since eclipsed about three dozen times). Also on the list was one of the most original works in the Western World's art canon: *The Arnolfini Portrait* by Netherlands painter Jan van Eyck in 1434, perpetrated with oils on three panels of oak boards.

The home team was represented by London painter and printmaker William Hogarth's *A Rake's Progress*, a comic-strip series of canvasses which pioneered sequential art in the 1700s; David Hockney, the only living artist on the list who was recognized for a composition of *Mr. and Mrs. Clark* that drew heavily on both *The Arnolfini Portrait* and *A Rake's Progress* to represent fashion designer Ossie Clark; and *The Hay Wain*, a large oil on canvas by John Constable celebrating the English rural life that had long been revered as one of England's greatest paintings.

In the end, the vote was not all that close. The winner was *The Fighting Téméraire Tugged to Her Last Berth to Be Broken Up*, 1838 painted by a contemporary and bitter rival of Constable, Joseph Mallord William Turner. If The Greatest Painting in Britain was a referendum on how Brits saw themselves in the 21st century, it was as a wistful people looking back on their days as the greatest naval power on earth.

The poll that attracted more than 110,000 votes could also be seen as a final coronation of the early 19th century painter himself. J.M.W. Turner was admired for his talent and technique, especially with watercolors and eventually oils as well, but seldom revered among his peers, who considered him crass of personality and lacking in proper breeding. Those were the critics who liked his work. The scolds who did not cater to his Romantic canvasses hated them all the more for the unpleasantness of the man who created them.

Not that Turner was one to clip out negative reviews and post them on his studio wall. He was secretive and prolific in his paintings and did more than any other artist to elevate landscape painting to the lofty status of historical painting that was universally held to be the highest form of Western painting. Turner knew his rightful place among the Old Masters; 150 years after his death, the people of England agreed with him.

Chapter 1: Early Life

The last time the sheep and cattle market town of South Molton in the Shire of Devon blazed prominently on English radar was in 1655. John Penruddock, who was a member of the Sealed Knot, a secret society of Royalists agitating for the Restoration of the Monarchy, selected South Molton as the place for him to lead the association's largest revolt. The Penruddock Uprising was easily put down in a few hours by Oliver Cromwell's troops, and for his troubles, the 36-year old Colonel's head was severed from the rest of his body. This is where Joseph Mallord William Turner's people lived.

His grandfather began shearing human heads as well as sheep's fleece, but there were not enough heads in South Molton for two barbers to prosper, so his son William set out from southwestern England to practice his trade in the big city of London in 1770. William Turner settled in the heart of London at 26 Maiden Lane in the working class district of Covent Garden, opening his barbering business and wig-making shop just a few blocks from the River Thames.

William, spare and muscular, had an engaging manner and great reserves of energy. He was gregarious and flashed an ever-present smile and quickly established an amiable presence for his business on Maiden Lane. Here the young haircutter met Mary Marshall, said to be a member of Shelford manor in Nottinghamshire with roots going back to King Henry II in the 12th century. By the 18th century, however, what privileges may have once accrued to her family had eroded. Mary had a brother who was a fishmonger on the docks of the North Sea at Margate, and another working as a butcher in Brentford west of London. On August 29, 1773 William Turner, aged 28, and Mary Marshall, who was a rare maiden to wed for the first time at age 34, were married at St. Paul's Cathedral, the masterwork of architect Sir Christopher Wren.

William and Mary's first child arrived on April 23, 1775, four days after the first shots were fired in the American colonies at Lexington and Concord. He was given the name of his mother's oldest brother, Joseph. A little sister was born in 1778 and named after her mother, but Mary Anne would die just days before her fifth birthday. Joseph Mallord William Turner would thereafter grow up as an only child.

It became apparent early on that young Joseph would not be following his relatives behind a counter in an English shop. Even before he entered school, he was demonstrating a talent for art by sketching out a coat-of-arms for a local jeweler from a set of castors, and at the age of nine he completed a detailed drawing of the church in his uncle's seaside town of Margate that was kept and treasured by a resident named John White. William told anyone who listened about his boy, "the artist."

Chapter 2: Education

At the age of ten, following an illness, Joseph went away from the city to school in Brentford, where he lived with his uncle the butcher. He was kept busy coloring engravings from Henry Boswell's recently released Antiquities of England and Wales for a local distiller who paid him a fourpence, a silver coin worth four pennies, per engraving. Copies of the engravings were sent to his father who put them for sale in his shop, where many of his customers were literary figures, actors, architects and painters who required their powdered wigs teased. The copied engravings and young Turner's own drawings sold well, enough so that William reluctantly gave up his dream of his son continuing in the family tradition of barbering and wig-making.

In 1786, young Turner was sent to a school on Soho Square to receive his first art instruction with a floral drawing master named Palice. He already seemed to be well beyond that point, being busily employed copying watercolors, coloring prints and making his own sketches. John Raphael Smith, a respected engraver and print seller, sent regular work to both Turner and a fellow fledgling artist two months his senior, Thomas Girtin. Turner and Girtin became friends who would in short time become flag bearers for the establishment of watercolor as a fine art form.

Sickly again at the age of 13 in 1788, Turner was sent back to the seacoast at Margate where he enrolled in school for about six months, the longest sustained formal education he would ever receive. The following year, back in London, he attended a school headmastered by Thomas Malton. Unable to keep up in math and geometry, Joseph was sent home as being "stupid and unteachable." Turner held no grudges but recognized his deficiencies with regards to practical learning; he would in later writings revel in his time as an architectural draftsman under Malton and refer to him as "my real master." Away from the classroom, Turner painted scenery for London theaters, where he picked up a lasting affection for opera and stage music.

All the while, Turner was doing work for local architects washing in skies and backgrounds to their drawings. Thomas Hardwick was so impressed with the young man's improvements to his architectural work that he advised Joseph to pursue a course as a landscape painter, and urged William to send his son to the Royal Academy Schools.

The Royal Academy of Arts had been founded by King George III in 1768, and rapidly became the country's leading society of artists. Classes were held in the sprawling Somerset House, that had been designed in a Neoclassical style by Sir William Chambers, overlooking the River Thames in central London. Turner was assigned to the studio of Sir Joshua Reynolds, a signal to all in the Academy that this was a lad of true talent.

Reynolds had been elected first President of the Royal Academy, and was acclaimed as the greatest English portraitist of the 18th century. Part of Turner's training was to copy some of Reynolds' famous portraits, including one of the great figure-painter himself. Turner's time under the influence of Sir Joshua was brief, as the master talent passed away at the age of 69 in 1792. Although he was kept busy with his portrait work, Reynolds always believed that history painting was the highest calling to which a painter could aspire, a conviction that was not lost on his young pupil.

By 1790, Turner was actively pursuing his craft as a landscape painter. He regularly set out on rambles of twenty and more miles in the countryside, hauling his sketchbook and pencils in a bundle slung over his shoulder on a stick. Having inherited his father's healthy constitution, Joseph was well-suited for such adventures. When he saw something that interested him, he stopped and started sketching. That same year he exhibited his first drawing at the Royal Academy of Arts, culled from his wanderings: *A View of the Archbishop's Palace at Lambeth*. In the next 60 years, exactly 267 paintings by J.M.W. Turner would hang on the Academy's walls.

In 1792, Turner received a commission from John Walker, an engraver and print seller, who began publishing *The Copper Plate Magazine* and the *Monthly Cabinet of Picturesque Prints* that year. *The Pocket Magazine* was another publication to which Turner was able to sell illustrations during his malleable teenage years. His touring became more extensive at this time, ranging into South Wales as he made pictures during his travels of cathedrals, bridges and townscapes. He was also beginning to feel the pull of the sea during his travels.

Turner also picked up a job making copies of works by the influential landscape painter John Robert Cozens. Cozens was the son of Russian-born watercolor and drawing master, Alexander Cozens, who had emigrated from St. Petersburg to London via Italy when in his thirties during the 1740s. After studying with his father, the young Cozens began to have his drawings exhibited in the Royal Academy while still in his teens. He made two trips to the European continent of several years' duration in his twenties that greatly influenced his work, as he imbued his landscapes with imaginative atmospheric effects that divided critical review of his work. Regardless of which side one fell on concerning Cozens' art, one of his renderings of Italy's Lake Albano from 1777 sold at auction in 2010 for more than two million dollars, more than any 18th century British watercolor has ever fetched.

In 1794, Cozens suffered a nervous breakdown at the age of 42 and was sent to Bethlem Royal Hospital for the insane. He was never to recover and was cared for by the asylum's chief physician and one-time consulting doctor to King George III, Thomas Munro, for the remaining three years of his life. Turner was called on to finish many of the unfinished landscapes Cozens left behind.

In addition to his doctoring, Munro was an amateur draftsman and patron of British artists. Both Turner and Thomas Girtin became members of "the Munro Circle," artists who gathered at the famed collector's country house near Leatherhead. Turner's exposure to the country's most celebrated watercolorists constituted one of the most formative episodes of his art education.

In addition to rubbing palettes with his contemporaries Turner was also starting to dip his brush back to painters of days gone by. He latched onto Richard Wilson from Montgomeryshire, Wales who was one of the earliest major British landscape artists. Wilson had spent time in Rome that informed his work with a palpable romanticism and a dramatic use of light. Despite the enormous influence Wilson's work would have on Turner, the Welsh artist found acceptance of his work elusive, and he was forced to take a position as librarian of the Royal Academy of Arts to ease his financial burden.

Turner's education as a topographic artist continued to expand as well with explorations in the Midlands in 1794, Yorkshire and the Lake District in 1797, and return trips to Wales. In 1796, Turner exhibited his first oil painting at the Royal Academy, Fishermen at Sea. Influenced by the nocturnal scenes of artists such as French war painter Philip de Loutherbourg and landscape specialist Joseph Wright of Derby, Turner depicted a fishing trawler negotiating the treacherous rocks off the Isle of Wight called the *Needles on a Cloudy Moonlit Night*.

To create his oils, Turner used the same techniques as his watercolors, building up from foundations of color that would morph into forms that would appear eerily aglow. In 1799, Turner, then 24 years old, was elected an associate of the Royal Academy, the youngest age that such a membership was allowed. It was also that year that J.M.W. Turner consulted his old friend and patron Dr. Thomas Munro on an affair not relating to his passion but to his profession.

Chapter 3: Early Career

Mary Turner had always been of quick temper, subject to ungovernable furies. In 1799, her impending insanity forced Mary to be sent to St. Luke's Hospital for Lunatiks that had been founded in 1751 as the second public institution devoted to the mentally ill in England. The next year she was admitted to the Bethlem Hospital and placed under the care of Dr. Munro.

Bethlem traces its roots to the year 1247 when it was set up to collect alms for the Holy Crusades. It instead became a house of the poor, and since the 1400s has been the oldest psychiatric hospital in the world. Even its popular name, "Bedlam," became a synonym for madness. Nothing could be done for Mary Turner in Bethlem, however, and she was discharged as incurable, living out the last years of her life in obscurity until dying in 1804.

Despite her troubles, Mary Turner and her only child had been able to share interests in times when she was in right mind. He undoubtedly inherited his artistic sensibilities from her and she was able to perform a sitting for a portrait. Although he reportedly never saw his mother again after she was forced from his life, Joseph could bear no reference to her for the remainder of his days.

By this time, Turner, with his quick ascension in the Royal Academy of Arts, was acknowledged to be one of the finest topographical watercolor artists practicing in England. Certifying that his "period of development" was indeed over, Turner moved to a tonier address at 64 Harley Street, setting up studio space with marine painter John Thomas Serres. Serres, just entering his forties, had been Master of Drawing at the Royal Naval College and the Maritime Painter to King George III in the 1790s. But after his wife Olivia decided she was the illegitimate daughter of the Earl of Cumberland and pressed her claims against King George in the House of Lords, Serres' royal patronage disappeared. His career in shambles, he would ultimately die in a London debtors' prison in 1825.

The career of his roommate, J.M.W. Turner, was moving in the opposite direction. Many considered Turner destined to be the finest painter of his generation, and his commission log book was full enough by his early twenties to guarantee a lifetime's income. Turner had acquired a coterie of rich aristocrats who were eager to form alliances with the brilliant prodigy. In 1802, he quietly assumed the gardens and outbuildings in the property on Harley Street. By 1803, Turner was the sole tenant.

About this time, William Turner went to live with his son and spent the remainder of his days working as an assistant in the studio, and serving as Joseph's agent in business matters if required. He would follow this routine until his death in his 84th year in 1829. More than once, William's light touch honed from decades of dealing with temperamental customers with unruly wigs would prove an asset on Harley Street.

J.M.W. Turner was notoriously secretive, allowing no one to see his work, and was seen as brash and arrogant, even among his legion of wealthy supporters. Turner never surrendered the Cockney accent he acquired on the working streets of London, and was often dismissed as being "uncouth" in the tonier circles of the British art world. "He had the manners of a groom, with no respect," snorted one pretentious contemporary.

In public lectures, Turner was unable to express his thoughts clearly and often fell to stuttering. Rather than be mocked for his Cockney speech, most often Turner would remain silent, promoting a suspicion of aloofness even more acutely. If he was ever to display a more loquacious side it was only among close friends, but even they were inclined to consider him grumpy and impenetrable.

Turner gained a reputation for a lack of generosity in appraising the works of his fellow artists. His ill-disguised disdain for those of inferior talents – which essentially covered all his contemporaries – led to bitter rivalries during his lifetime. In 1802, his teenage friend Thomas Girtin, who had moved professionally away from Turner, succumbed to a disease described as "ossification of the heart" and died at the age of 27. Although estranged in recent years, Turner attended the funeral and erected a tombstone in Girtin's honor in the Covent Garden churchyard. He was reported to have said, "Had Tom Girtin lived, I should have starved."

Having worked from the age of 12 - whether it was pushing paintings on customers queueing up for a shave, painting backgrounds in an opera house, or giving an art lesson for a few shillings - Joseph Mallord William Turner knew what it was like to hustle a buck. And his need for money would become permanently ingrained in his character, a trait that seldom meshed in the snobbish world of art. After squeezing top dollar for commissions from his patrons, Turner was known to ask for "extra monies" to cover the cost of the frame.

Sir Walter Scott, Scottish historical novelist and poet of such titles as *Rob Roy* and *Ivanhoe*, once hired Turner for some engravings of the Edinburgh countryside. Afterward, the writer described his dealings with the painter in a letter to a friend: "Turner's palm is as itchy as his fingers are ingenious. He will do nothing without cash, and anything for it. He is the only man of genius I ever knew who is sordid in these matters." Of course, Scott grew up ensconced in the comfort of the Tory establishment, and never knew what it was like to want for a dollar or worry where the next may come from.

While Turner's personality did not meld readily into the crusty British art scene it had the advantage of making it easy for the artist to keep his private and professional lives separate, as he wished. Early on, Turner decided never to marry. "I hate married men," he opined. "They never make any sacrifice to the arts but are always thinking of their duty to their wives and their families, or some rubbish of that sort."

Not that J.M.W. Turner was ever wanting for female companionship. He would enjoy it, albeit simply ignoring the "rubbish" that came along in its wake. Even into his seventies, Turner would fill his sketchbooks with erotic renderings that included close-up drawings of the act of copulation. His love life was far from an open book, and at best, his close friends knew nothing of Turner's flirtations.

In 1798, or thereabouts, he took up with Sarah Danby, the wife of a musician friend who had recently died. Turner's affair with the widow Danby, ten years his senior, would last, off and on, for 15 years. With his burgeoning wealth, he was able to set Danby up in a home of her own which was convenient since the relationship produced two illegitimate daughters, Evelina and Georgiana, about whom nothing was ever known in Turner's lifetime. Their existence became public only after modest stipends were made in their names in the artist's will.

As for his own household on Harley Street Turner retained the services of one of Danby's relatives, an unmarried woman named Hannah who came to work for the artist and his father when she was 23 years old. She would cook and keep the Turner house for 40 years until his death. And that is how J.M.W. Turner set up his life, free to give his full attention to his art.

Turner supplemented his move to more fashionable quarters and increased renown by increasing his travel schedule. He made it to Scotland in 1801, and in 1802, made his first crossing to continental Europe. His boat trip to Calais on the north coast of France was harrowing and he captured the experience in his picture Calais Pier. Turner portrayed a packet boat burdened with passengers rocked by high swells under dark storm clouds. In his sketchbook for the picture, Turner's notation indicated the seas were so rough he was "nearly swampt." Turner first displayed the oil on canvas in the Royal Academy in 1803 to harsh reviews, many believing the foreground was not yet finished. Calais Pier today hangs in the National Gallery on Trafalgar Square in London.

On his first trip to Europe, Turner made more than 400 drawings of his explorations in France and Switzerland that would fuel his work back on Harley Street for years. While in Paris he indulged in a study of the Old Masters on display in the Louvre. Turner was especially taken by the history paintings of Nicolas Poussin who had founded the French classical tradition in the early 1600s, but had fallen out of favor in the 1700s.

Also of interest were the landscapes of 17th century French artist Claude Lorrain. Lorrain was regarded at that time as the one master of landscape painting, and his poetic idealization of his countrysides and transformative rendering of light would influence Turner's work throughout his career. He pulled the same lyrical use of light and atmosphere from the naturalistic works of Dutch Baroque painter Aelbert Cuyp. The Englishman's reputation as "painter of the light" began to take hold with this very first trip to Europe.

Back in England in 1802, Turner was elected to be a full member of the Royal Academy of Arts. Dripping with new importance, his name appeared in the Academy catalog for the first time as Joseph Mallord William Turner. Before that it had been listed as J.W. Turner or W. Turner. At his home growing up he was always called "William" by his parents.

In 1804, Turner opened a gallery down the street from his home and studio at the corner of Harley and Queen Anne Streets. The space could display up to 30 works comfortably in contrast to the crowded walls at the Royal Academy. Turner filled his new gallery with watercolors fleshed out from the drawings of his European trip. He rapidly accumulated a new bevy of patrons including Walter Ramsden Hawkesworth Fawkes, a prominent Yorkshire landowner and Member of Parliament.

Fawkes came to allow Turner an open invitation at his Farnley Hall estate, and over the years, the artist would spend months at a time on the grounds, sketching and painting, almost every year from 1808 until the nobleman's death in 1825. In 1819, Fawkes opened his London house to an exhibition of his collection of more than 70 Turners; today, the Turner collection at Farnley Hall consists of some 200 of the painter's finest works.

While Turner's talent was being hailed in ever-widening circles, the acclaim was far from universal. The luminescence of Turner's canvasses led some to deride his light-centric pictures as the work of a "white painter", and others considered his topographic interpretations to be pale imitations of earlier landscape painters. Benjamin West, born in the American colonies near Springfield, Pennsylvania, who became one of the first American artists to be feted in Europe, called some of the paintings exhibited in Turner's gallery "crude botches" during his stint as President of the Royal Academy.

While not oblivious to the slights, the occasional criticism did little to crack the artist's thick veneer of self-confidence. As his career progressed, he even came to deliberately invite adverse reaction to controversial paintings. As for attacks from fellow members of the Academy, Turner never wavered in his loyalty to the organization, referring to it as the "mother of artists." In 1808, after discovering the Academy was having difficulty filling the post of Professor of Perspective, he proposed himself for the job. Proud of his new position, Turner took to adding the initials "P.P." to his customary "R.A." after signing his name.

As a professor, it would be three years before Turner felt comfortable enough to begin delivering lectures to the polished audiences of the Academy in his thick Cockney accent. Even those who found his delivery coarse conceded that the content of his research and the illustrations he had prepared were worthy of praise. Turner kept the cherished post for thirty years, even though he stopped lecturing in the 1820s.

By this time, Turner was less concerned with comparisons to contemporary artists than how he stacked up against the Old Masters. Claude Lorrain had made a sketchbook of 195 drawings of the compositions of his paintings as a way to record his creations and protect against forgeries. He called the seminal work *Liber Veritas* (the Book of Truths) and added to it from 1635 until 1682. In 1807, Turner decided to undertake his own studio record to catalog the growing variety of his own work, which had expanded to include his original approach to seascapes as well as landscapes. He called his series *Liber Studiorum* and set out to create 100 plates. After a dozen years, however, he wearied of the project and abandoned it with only 71 completed.

Turner would never let go of his presumed rivalry with those Old Masters who influenced his style. He first exhibited *Sun Rising Through Vapour: Fishermen Cleaning and Selling Fish* in the Royal Academy in 1807, but was so acutely aware of its place in his personal development that when he donated it to the National Gallery 35 years later, he did so with the proviso that it hang between two masterpieces the gallery owned by French master Claude Gellée.

As his thirties wound down, Turner amped up the atmospheric qualities of his paintings by relying more and more on the effects of light. He experimented with layering of dark and light watercolors to create expressionistic forms that the artist enhanced by scraping, blotting and wiping the paint while it was still wet. Many of the artistic elements that found their way onto Turner's canvasses stood in stark opposition to conventional theory, giving Turner's critics fertile ground for further derision.

In 1811, Turner went on tour in the West Country to collect subjects for a series of engravings based on England's south coast that would be reminiscent of the classical seaports depicted by the Old Masters. The next year, he exhibited a light-bathed *St. Mawes at the Pilchard Season*, capturing in oil the defensive role the fishing port was assuming in the Napoleonic Wars. The seaside adventure yielded material that would comprise *Picturesque Views on the Southern Coast of England* which was assembled between 1814 and 1826. The 48 plates and 32 engraved vignettes were produced by William Bernard Cooke and his younger brother George. It was the most important work for these esteemed line engravers who specialized in marine views.

The book was published by the house of John Murray, founded by the man whose name appeared on the letterhead in 1768. His son, John Murray II, built the firm into the most influential book producer in England by bringing out the works of Lord Byron, Jane Austen and Washington Irving, the first successful American novelist. In later years, John Murray would publish Charles Darwin's *The Origin of Species* and Sir Arthur Conan Doyle. Picturesque Views on the Southern Coast of England was the first substantial series of Turner's topographical watercolors, and proved to be a boon to, most importantly, his bank account and to his reputation secondarily.

He followed it up with an ambitious survey of England's rivers, ports and harbors entitled Picturesque Views in England and Wales. Charles Heath, who was the first to mass-produce steel engravings in England, handled the production work beginning in 1827. The project did not sell well enough to continue to completion, and was abandoned in 1838, but further burnished Turner's reputation as a recorder of early nineteenth-century England.

Turner's draw to the water was more than professional. He often took temporary lodgings along the Thames River to indulge his favorite hobby: fishing. The Thames historically had been the province of poets and painters but by the early 1800s, the shores were becoming increasingly developed by the expanding industrial age and Turner felt a responsibility to convey the cultural history of the riverside. In 1807, he purchased a bit of the Thames shoreline for himself in Twickenham.

In 1813, Turner designed and built a villa he called Solus Lodge at 40 Sandycoombe Road. From this retreat, the leading naturalist painter of his day sketched the mother river of England in watercolor and oil. Turner sold the cottage, now known as Sandycombe Lodge, in 1826. Today, it is the only surviving building designed by Turner, although it is precariously listed on the English Heritage at Risk register.

In 1812, Turner visited one of his favorite themes in examining man's vulnerability when stacked against the forces of nature. In this case he documented one of history's most notable military achievements: Punic commander Hannibal taking his army across the Alps, in the face of bitter winter conditions. After its exhibition, *Snow Storm: Hannibal and His Army Crossing the Alps* turned out to be one of Turner's most popular history painting canvasses. Turner had made a habit of appending snippets of quotes to his paintings from his favorite poets since 1798, but with *Snow Storm: Hannibal and His Army Crossing the Alps* he used selections from a poem he himself had written, "Fallacies of Hope." Excerpts from Turner's verse would show up with various paintings over the years, but the poem was never finished nor published.

In 1814, Turner took to painting an historical series based on the civilization of Ancient Carthage that thrived between 650 BC and 146 BC. His first picture to reach exhibit in 1814 was *Leaving Carthage on the Morning of the Chase* which was a visual interpretation of Virgil's Latin poem "The Aeneid." In the tale, Prince Aeneas, whose destiny is to found Rome, flees Troy at the end of the Trojan War and shipwrecks on the North African coast near Carthage. While waiting for transportation out of Africa Aeneas falls in love with the Carthage queen, Dido. He delays leaving for Italy as long as he responsibly can, but when he ultimately leaves the heartbroken Dido takes her life in grief. Turner depicts the couple in happier times, leading a hunting expedition into the woods. For his series on Carthage, Turner unearthed works by Lord Byron, John Milton and William Shakespeare to emphasize the literary-historical import of his artistic interpretations.

With the fires of the Napoleonic Wars exhausted in 1815, Turner traveled back to the Continent, taking tours of Holland and Belgium and the Rhineland. He went to see the battlefield at Waterloo where only months earlier, on June 18, coalition armies from six nations ended Napoleon Bonaparte's rule as Emperor of France. After 22 years of war, there was too long a trudge of loss and suffering from the Napoleonic campaigns for excessive rejoicing. Certainly Turner's The Field of Waterloo, first exhibited in 1818, made no display of flag-waving. The canvas is unrelentingly dark, and the only light illuminates survivors searching through piles of dead bodies in hopes of locating loved ones. The painting was interpreted as an allegory for the depravities of war rather than the celebration of a single battle.

In the summer of 1819, Turner packed his crates again for a return expedition to Europe, under happier circumstances. This time he was headed for Italy, his first trip into the heart of Renaissance painting. He spent more than three months in Rome, allowing time to take in the artistic wonders of Florence, Naples and Venice as well. Turner executed some 1,500 drawings during his time in Italy, providing material for years of work.

Rome, from the Vatican. Raffaele, Accompanied by La Fornarina, Preparing his Pictures for the Decoration of the Loggia, an oil on canvas, was representative of his Italian inspiration. Exhibited in 1820 and created at the height of his power, the canvas captures all that Rome meant to him, looking at the city from the Vatican loggia as it stretches out across St. Peter's Square and onto the Abruzzi Hills. In a nod to his romantic predecessors, Raphael can be seen in the foreground.

At this point in his career, Turner was experimenting with purer colors in his oils and juxtaposing vibrant shadow against his iridescent light. When *The Bay of Baiae, with Apollo and the Sibyl* was exhibited in 1823, it demonstrated the golden hues of the landscape against the Bay of Naples. The setting is the backdrop for the tragic myth of Sibyl, a mortal, who was coveted by the god Apollo. In exchange for her virginity she asked to live for as long as the number of grains of sand she held in her hand. When she came to refuse Apollo, he kept his end of the bargain and allowed Sibyl to live for one thousand years. But since she never requested eternal youth, Apollo allowed for her body to grow smaller with age until all that remained was her voice.

With his usual book of commissions and backlog of material gleaned from Italy, the 1820s were a busy time for Turner as he continued his travels to continental Europe and the countryside in England and Scotland. In 1826, he returned to France with intentions to paint the great rivers of Europe. The project never materialized, but it did yield three volumes of prints published by Charles Heath that aimed at a more middle class market where some might actually aspire to such artistic pretensions, culled together as *Rivers of France*. In 1828 it was Italy again, this time entirely in Rome where Turner painted and also exhibited new works.

Turner's great patron, Walter Fawkes, passed away in 1825. Fawkes had interested his good friend, George O'Brien Wyndham, the 3rd Earl of Egremont, in Turner's work and the Earl became a Turner friend and patron as well. After Fawkes' death, he never returned to Farnley Hall again, but became a regular visitor to the Earl's seat at Petworth House. Turner even kept a studio in the Old Library on the upper floor.

Turner had done his first painting of Petworth back in 1809 during a visit to the countryside with artist acquaintances. Now he painted the mansion, landscapes and the Chichester Ship Canal, a pet project of Wyndham's. *Petworth: the White Library, looking down the Enfilade from the Alcove*, executed in 1827, shows the interior of the country house in watercolor and pen and ink. Turner worked on four paintings destined for the Carved Room in Petworth that looked out towards a lake. The most famous of these became the oil on canvas, *Chichester Canal*, composed in 1828. The Earl was in his mid-seventies in the 1820s, and Turner would maintain a presence at Petworth until O'Brien died in 1837 at the age of 85.

The 1820s ended with the death of William Turner, leaving J.M.W. Turner without family for the first time. Only a month into the new decade, Thomas Lawrence, the successor to Benjamin West as the President of the Royal Academy of Arts, died. Whereas his predecessor had vacillated on his judgment of Turner, Lawrence left no room for interpretation with his appraisal: "J.M.W. Turner is indisputably the first landscape painter in Europe."

Lawrence was himself the premiere portraitist of the time, celebrated across Europe for capturing the personalities of royalty, politicians and military leaders on canvas. Honors overflowed his studio, including Principal Painter-in-Ordinary to the King. He had been President of the Royal Academy of Arts since 1820 and always generous to Turner. He wrote letters of introduction recommending Turner's "genius" to contacts in Europe, and owned several Turners himself.

It was through the machinations of Thomas Lawrence and his connections with the Royal Court that secured J.M.W. Turner's only Royal Commission. *The Battle of Trafalgar, 21 October 1805* was completed during the years 1823-24 for King George IV. Turner compressed many of the events of the battle into a single canvas which drew criticism from literalists but he was again intending to use his oils to portray the symbolic cost of victory, not the heroics of victory. Turner loads his foreground with dead and dying sailors who sacrificed their lives for the British naval victory over France.

When Turner drew up his first will in 1829, he endowed a chair and a gold medal for landscape painting in a show of backing for Lawrence. After the Academy president's unexpected passing at the age of 61, a stunned Turner wrote to Charles Lock Eastlake, another Academician, "Do but think what a loss we and the arts have in the death of Sir Thomas Lawrence."

England had not seen a funeral with an outpouring of pomp and circumstance such as Lawrence's precipitated since that exhibited at the procession for Admiral Horatio Nelson, after the national hero had been shot and killed in that Battle of Trafalgar a quarter-century earlier. The night before the ceremony, Lawrence's body lay in repose in Somerset House at the Royal Academy, and so many people squeezed into the streets the next day to view the velvet-draped coffin pass by that the newly-established Metropolitan Police Force was given one of their first assignments to control crowds. Curiously, many of the estimated 80 elaborately outfitted carriages in the procession were actually empty, sent as a gesture of respect by the nobility. That was common practice in the 19th century, when funerals were typically only attended by immediate family. Still, Turner disapproved of the empty carriages in this case, especially as many of those owners had sat for cherished Lawrence portraits through the years.

Those who could not attend the spectacle could read about it in exhausting detail in the next day's London Times or view *Funeral of Sir Thomas Lawrence: A Sketch from Memory* that Turner created in tribute and exhibited later in the year. Turner's watercolor portrays the arrival of Lawrence's coffin at the Great West Door of St. Paul's Cathedral, having been delivered by a shiny black horse-drawn hearse. Mourners are trailing the coffin, walking as pairs into the famous dome. The strings of January sunshine wash the great space with a particular melancholy.

So as it was in his 55th year, Joseph Mallord William Turner would be looking at the remainder of his life without his most illustrious contemporary professional advocate, without the father who had been a steadying presence in his life and who promoted his work for more than four decades, and without his most enthusiastic patron in Walter Fawkes.

Chapter 4: Later Life and Career

While J.M.W. Turner may have had his personal and professional foundations shaken as he entered the latter stages of his career he certainly had his widespread fame and wealth to sustain him. Turner's work in his fifties cast away assiduous observations of architectural fidelity and careful natural observation in favor of greater attention to light and color. His exhibitions featured his highly salable classical subjects from history but also more abstract works as well.

But the master historical artist was still quick to grasp the symbolic value of current events around him. As clocks around London wound towards seven o'clock on the night of October 16, 1834, the Houses of the Lords and Commons burst into flame, consuming adjacent buildings as well. From the south bank of the River Thames, Turner, along with tens of thousands of spectators, observed the conflagration. As the flames continued to lick the dark London night, Turner rented a small skiff to float onto the river and study the unnatural light more closely.

It was scarcely lost on Turner and others that the destruction of the Houses of Parliament took place less than two years following the Reform Act 1832, that shifted seats in the House of Commons to cities engorged by the Industrial Revolution and away from the landed gentry, increasing the number of individuals eligible to vote, and greasing the skids for a more democratic England. Turner set to work to evoke the changing political landscape on canvas.

He produced a series of pictures, and after working and reworking two oil on canvas paintings sent one to the British Institution the following February and the other to the Royal Academy of Arts in the summer. The first, *The Burning of the Houses of Lords and Commons, October 16, 1834*, depicts the chamber of the House of Commons in St. Stephen's Chapel, the core of which had built in a Gothic style in 1297 and converted to government use in 1547, completely engulfed in flames. The towers of Westminster Abbey, that will survive the blaze, appear as a spectral image through the golden fire. The flames flick against the Westminster Bridge that dominates the foreground.

The Burning of the Houses of Lords and Commons, October 16, 1834 that was exhibited at the Royal Academy provided a perspective of the fire from downstream near the Waterloo Bridge. From this viewpoint, Turner evoked the drama through the eyes of spectators on shore and in boats on the Thames. Both of the evocative historical accounts reside today in the United States; the first has been in the Philadelphia Museum of Art since 1928, and the second was acquired by the Cleveland Museum of Art in 1942.

If the burning of the House of Parliament was reflective of the destruction of the old guard of British politics, Turner was also witness to an equally symbolic, and for the master marine painter of his day, more poignant passing of an age. One day in 1838 he saw an old warship, the Téméraire, being pulled upstream to a salvage yard by a steam-powered tug. He painted an elegy to the passing of the era of sailing ships in *The Fighting Téméraire Tugged to Her Last Berth to Be Broken Up, 1838*.

Turner used the ship's nickname for his oil painting on canvas. The HMS Téméraire was launched in 1798 with full rigging and 98 guns. She sailed into action in the Napoleonic Wars but saw no fighting of consequence until the Battle of Trafalgar in 1805 when she came to the rescue of the Admiral Horatio Nelson's besieged flagship, HMS Victory, and captured two French warships. The heroic actions of its crew earned her the nickname "The Fighting Téméraire" and the resolute love of a grateful nation.

After repairs "The Fighting Téméraire" was deployed routinely as a blockader of ports and a support vessel, occasionally engaging in minor gun battles. After 1813, she served as a prison ship for many years and then in increasingly insignificant duties until the British Admiralty sold her for scrap in 1838. She was towed in ignominy to Rotherhithe to be broken up board by board. Turner painted her final voyage as a tribute to the glories of the HMS Téméraire's early days, but he left no doubt that the magical days of sailing ships and indeed England's superiority at sea, upon which the British Empire was built, were riding on her decks on that day as well. The Thames is set against a dramatic sunset, even though The Téméraire's journey was in reality moving in the opposite direction. The great ship itself is a ghostly figure with only the steam-spewing tugboat showing any life. The sense of loss is palpable as the procession on the River Thames plays out.

J.M.W. Turner was in his sixties when *The 'Fighting Téméraire' Tugged to Her Last Berth to Be Broken Up, 1838* was painted. The technical mastery of his strokes was praised - the laying on of thick layers of paint to send the last rays of the setting sun through the low clouds in contrast to the exacting brushstrokes of the ship's rigging, for instance. But aside from the technique, the power of the artistry is what endures. That is what struck a chord with the public more than 175 years later when of *The 'Fighting Téméraire' Tugged to Her Last Berth to Be Broken Up, 1838* was voted Britain's favorite painting.

Turner was far from a Luddite when it came to the Industrial Revolution that was changing Europe faster in decades than it had evolved in the hundreds of years prior combined. He was fascinated by the advancement wrought by steam machines, and in the early 1840s he composed *Rain, Steam, and Speed – the Great Western Railway*. Looking east to London a powerful train steams across the Maidenhead railway bridge. Turner captures the speed of the new "Iron Horse," bringing not just passengers in the open cars towards the viewer but an entirely new way of life. A small rabbit, a helpless nature in symbolism perhaps, caught on the tracks is scrambling to get out of the way of this new and unstoppable force.

One of the things Turner pursued in the twilight of his career was more of a leadership role in his profession. Even as he divested himself of his dormant professorship at the Royal Academy of Arts, he was taking on more responsibility, joining committees and advocating a farewell dinner for the Somerset House when the venerable building was abandoned for newer digs in 1836. On his frequent trips to the Continent, Turner was now occasionally putting down his sketchbook to study architectural drawings in the pursuit of a new building for the Academy. He made a stop in Berlin to look in on the Altes Museum ("Old Museum" in German) that Prussian architect and city planner Karl Friedrich Schinkel had designed for the royal art collection. The Neoclassical confection that was built between 1823 and 1830 was considered to represent the pinnacle of Schinkel's career.

Chapter 5: Joseph Mallord William Turner and John Ruskin

Even as he was continuing to produce acclaimed work in his advanced years, Turner was never far from his critics. One of the more eye-catching attacks appeared in Blackwood's *Edinburgh Magazine* following a Turner exhibition of Venetian works in 1835. The author was the Reverend John Eagles, nine years Turner's junior and no fan of the recently passed 1832 political reforms. If anything, Eagles was more conservative than the far-right journal for which he was writing. He was a landscape watercolorist himself who had been turned down for membership in The Watercolour Society when he was 25 years old, back in 1809.

Eagles also translated ancient Greek hymns, and did political writing for the magazine as well, a breadth of experience he felt made him uniquely qualified to take down his favorite target, Joseph Mallord William Turner. He began his criticism by revisiting the bromides about Turner's love of garish colors, and launched into a broadside on the artist himself. "Why, for the sake of this trickery fame, will Turner persist in throwing the gauze of flimsy novelty over his genius, great as it is. Is it that he would rest his fame on what he has done, and thus mislead, that he may have no rival in the British school thereafter?"

After accusing Turner of purposeful deceit in a vain attempt to cling to his popularity, Eagles then picked out a single work, *Juliet and Her Nurse*, for particular disdain, describing the painting as "…a composition as from different parts of Venice, thrown higgledy-piggledy together, streaked blue and pink and thrown into a flour tub…"

None of these apoplectic bursts made an impact on Turner whatsoever. He long ago grew hardened to critics, certainly those whose artistic talent he did not consider first rank. But the Eagles attack did inflame the passions of an unknown 17-year old student who had just matriculated at the University of Oxford.

John Ruskin was destined to become the most famous and influential art critic of the Victorian Age whose words would continue to reverberate through World War I. His father, a well-to-do importer of fine sherry, seemed to sense that future from the beginning. When he was just three years old, James Northcote was commissioned to do a series of portraits for the Ruskins. After he saw the painting of himself, young John suggested the addition of some small hills in the background because the portrait lacked visual interest.

At the age of ten his father informed him that, "You may be doomed to enlighten a People by your Wisdom & to adorn an age by your learning." Ruskin seemed to take the words to hear as other boys might if they were told to go out and play in the woods. The following year he saw his first Turner, *Vesuvius in Eruption*, a watercolor produced on slightly textured cream wove paper. There was a fascination with volcanoes in early 19th century Europe, and Turner was not immune to the phenomenon. In 1815, he exhibited *The Eruption of the Souffrier Mountains, in the Island of St. Vincent* which led his old publisher W.B. Cooke to paint Mount Vesuvius on the west coast of Italy.

Vesuvius was a favorite of naturalists and topographic artists. It had growled to life in 1794, and again in 1807, and would explode twice in the five years after Turner finished his renderings of the volcano. Turner was tasked to create companion watercolors, one with the volcano at rest and another with the basaltic mountain spitting molten rocks. Turner was still two years away from his first travels to Italy so he would have had to have worked from drawings of others, a subtle fact that an 11-year old John Ruskin could not have known when he became hooked for life by Turner's "scrupulous faithfulness to nature."

For his 13th birthday, his father's business partner gave John an edition of Samuel Roger's poem *Italy* that contained 25 of Turner's engraved vignettes which the boy treasured and studied in equal parts. An artist of considerable talent himself, Ruskin began emulating the master's black and white line engravings in his own drawings. Although only 17, John Ruskin had been formulated opinions for many years of J.M.W. Turner and they were formidable.

Ruskin crafted a spirited rebuttal to the criticism of the Reverend Eagles, but his father cautioned his son that it might be a better course of action to send the screed to the artist first before submitting it to Blackwood's. This Ruskin did and he elicited a response from Turner: "I beg to thank you for your zeal, kindness, and the trouble you have taken in regard of the criticism of Blackwood's Magazine for October, respecting my works; but I never move in these matters."

It is not known if Turner reacted with the same disinterest to Blackwood's several years earlier, when the magazine tabbed him as the greatest landscape artist to stand before an easel since Claude. Turner's disinterest in responding to critics led Ruskin to return his comments to his desk, and the article would not be published in his lifetime. But it did lead to further correspondence between Turner and Ruskin which was to deeply impact the British art world. Turner would be a guest in the Ruskin home, and in 1839 the Ruskins bought their first drawing by Turner. John Ruskin would live for the remainder of the 19th century, dying at the age of 80. In his lifetime, he would own some 300 Turners at one time or another.

In 1843 Ruskin would announce himself to the art world with the publication of *Modern Painters*, the first of five volumes that would stretch until 1860. The first volume was almost exclusively a defense of J.M.W. Turner. Ruskin argued that the work of Britain's current picturesque painters, specifically Turner, was superior to the Old Masters in their landscape canvasses. Front and center among Turner's recent works effusively promoted by Ruskin was *Slave Ship* (*Slavers Throwing Overboard the Dead and Dying, Typhoon Coming On*), more commonly known as *The Slave Ship* when it was exhibited in 1840. Slavery had been outlawed in the British Empire in 1833 but was still a vibrant business in places in Europe like Spain and, of course, in the United States.

Turner read *The History and Abolition of the Slave Trade*, an 1808 exposé by Thomas Clarkson, which described an incident in 1781 where the master of the slave ship Zong ordered 133 slaves herded overboard in order to collect insurance payments. By 1840, Turner and a growing cadre of abolitionists believed it was time for slavery to end worldwide. He planned a canvas for the first ever meeting of the World Anti-Slavery scheduled to be staged over two weeks that summer in London's Exeter Hall. Turner placed his "Slave Ship" in the canvas sailing away from the eye of the viewer, towards the back. As it moves toward a blood-red sunset, dark figures with their hands in chains are seen bobbing in the coppery waters. The fate of the slaves is sealed by gathering sea creatures. Turner never shied away from difficult subjects, and never feared making his audience uncomfortable. Turner once again tapped his unpublished verse, "Fallacies of Hope" from 1812, for emphasis.

The impact of *The Slave Ship* on the convention is not gauged but in 1843, the British passed laws promising to be more vigilant against the slave trade which led to a rush of anti-slavery laws in other countries. In *Modern Painters* Ruskin gushed that *The Slave Ship* was the greatest "protest" painting in Turner's long career. He wrote, "I believe if I were reduced to rest Turner's immortality upon any single work, I should choose this. Its daring conception, ideal in the highest sense of the word, is based on the purest truth."

Ruskin let it be known that he hoped his father would find it in his heart to purchase *Slave Ship* (*Slavers Throwing Overboard the Dead and Dying, Typhoon Coming On*) which he in fact did, and presented it to John on New Year's Day 1844 as a reward for producing *Modern Painters*. The oil painting assumed a place of honor in the Ruskin dining room where the artist himself enjoyed more than one meal, but never once saw fit to mention the canvas. It was unseen by the public - who knew nothing of the work beyond Ruskin's excited descriptions - until the critic made a private sale of *The Slave Ship* to J.T. Johnston, a collector from the United States. The romantic maritime painting now hangs in the Museum of Fine Arts, Boston.

Another example Ruskin singled out for proof of Turner's genius was *Snow Storm – Steam-Boat off a Harbour's Mouth making Signals in Shallow Water, and going by the Lead. The Author was in this Storm on the Night the Ariel left Harwich*, an oil that Turner exhibited in 1842. Both the painting and the backstory sparked controversy. No account of such an incident in Harwich could be recalled, and many just assumed Turner had mis-remembered the name of the ship. Turner also claimed that the crew had lashed him to the main mast for four hours so that he could observe the squall at the height of its ferocity. That was even less believable but the artist maintained his position, even in private.

Critics of the work itself dismissed the canvas as nothing more than "soapsuds and whitewash" which Turner was said to have reacted at to at Ruskin's house by muttering, "Soapsuds and whitewash! What would they have? I wonder what they think the sea's like? I wish they'd been in it."

Ruskin's evaluation of the sea picture in Modern Painters was somewhat different. He called Turner's choices, "Three of the very finest pieces of colour that have come from his hand." He concluded by describing Snow Storm as "one of the very grandest statements of sea-motion, mist, and light, that has ever been put on canvas, even by Turner. Of course it was not understood; his finest works never are."

Chapter 6: Last Works

Joseph Mallord William Turner would have less than a decade to live when *Modern Painters* was published but it insured that he would spend his final years bathing in high public esteem. "Venice was surely built to be painted by ... Turner," concluded the Art Union upon seeing *The Dogano, San Giorgio, Citella, from the Steps of the Europa*. Rather than dwell on what Venice once was, Turner portrayed the city as he saw it with the water and light playing on stupendous Renaissance architecture.

John Ruskin even commissioned a painting from Turner, casting himself in the role of patron in addition to being defender and main cheerleader for his artistic hero. *The Pass of St. Gotthard, near Faido* was a graphite, watercolor and pen confection on paper. As he had done for the better part of five decades, Turner prepared for a major work by going on location and making pencil sketches. Switzerland was a favorite destination in his latter continental travels, and the detour to the high mountain pass in the Swiss Alps was no inconvenience.

St. Gotthard is a steep-sided gorge, and the pass was not used until the 13th century due to dangerous travel conditions in the winter, and excessive snowmelt in the spring and summer. When a daring bridge was constructed across the turbulent Reuss River in the pass, legend has it that it became a reality because a herdsman was losing so many sheep trying to cross the deadly waters that he swore to the Devil himself to build a bridge. The Devil did appear and agreed to the construction job in exchange for the soul of the first being to cross the bridge. The mountain man pondered the offer and ultimately agreed to the deal. After the bridge was made the herdsman drove a goat across ahead of himself.

Enraged by the this bit of rule-bending the Devil showed up in the St. Gotthard Pass with a massive boulder determined to smash the bridge to bits. But before he had a chance to shatter the bridge, an old woman hastily drew a cross on the gargantuan granite so the Devil could not budge it. For centuries, the Devil's Bridge could be used only by foot traffic but, by the time Turner arrived it had been improved to accept carriage traffic. The 220-ton rock still resides in the pass, and in 1977, the government spent 300,000 Swiss francs to move the boulder about 350 feet to make room for a new concrete bridge above the Devil's Bridge.

Ruskin was always vocal about his disapproval of artists who finished natural landscapes in the studio rather than "plein air", as was Turner's wont, but the master's studio finishes were so atmospheric he excluded his idol from such criticism. In the case of *The Pass of St. Gotthard, near Faido*, Ruskin was so smitten that he said about the painting, "He realized it for me in 1843, with his fullest power and the resultant drawing is, I believe, the greatest work he produced in the last period of his art." In 1845, Ruskin even made a special journey to Switzerland to see St. Gotthard Pass for himself.

Also in 1845, a Turner picture made its first appearance in America. The patron was James Lenox, a private collector from New York City who was the only son of a wealthy Scottish merchant who had set up shop along Fifth Avenue in the early 1800s. Young James studied law and was admitted to the New York Bar after graduating from what is today Columbia University, but he never bothered to put out a law shingle. When his father died that was enough of the business world for the younger Lenox as well.

For the last half century of his life, he devoted his time to building a library and gallery of paintings that were unsurpassed in North America. He certainly had the financial resources; at the time, there were said to be 19 millionaires in New York, and only a couple were considered richer than Lenox.

The deep-pocketed collector knew J.M.W. Turner by reputation but had only seen etchings of his work in books. So Lenox dispatched his friend Charles Robert Leslie with 500 pounds to bring him back a Turner. Leslie was a painter himself, born in London to American parents. He cultivated high-powered friendships on both sides of the Atlantic Ocean; he was raised in Philadelphia, but entered the Royal Academy of Arts in London in his twenties.

After calling on Turner's gallery to see what was on hand that could be bought for £500, Leslie picked out an atmospheric maritime picture of Fingal's Cave, a sea cave on the uninhabited Scottish island of Staffa in the Inner Hebrides. Turner painted the oil on canvas in 1832. The previous year, Turner had been hired by esteemed Edinburgh publisher Robert Cadell to cobble together illustrations for a collection of Sir Walter Scott's poems. Turner visited Scott, then in his declining years.

Scott called the remote island "one of the most extraordinary places I ever beheld." After taking his leave from the great poet, Turner decided to see for himself, boarding a steamer for his adventure. During his voyage, the ship was caught in a rollicking storm which Turner was able to translate to canvas in one of his favorite themes - man's humbling circumstances when faced with the unbridled power of nature. The sun makes its appearance only by bursting "through the rain-cloud-angry" to illuminate the harrowed steamship.

Turner exhibited Staffa, Finegal Cave to critical acclaim in 1832 but the picture had resided in his studio for more than a decade. It seemed like a perfect choice for Lenox - a strong representative of Turner's naturalistic painting, and a dramatic rendering of the Lenox ancestral lands to boot. Leslie packaged up Staffa and sent it across the sea with a note of explanation identifying the picture as "a most poetic picture of a steam boat."

Lenox could not have been more displeased when the Turner arrived on his doorstep. He sent word back to England that he was "greatly disappointed" by what he called the "indistinctness of the painting." Turner lore maintains that when Leslie relayed the American's opinion to him his response was, "You should tell Mr. Lenox that indistinctness is my forte."

Whether he delivered such a tart retort is open to conjecture, but it is known that he did send word to Lenox that he might be more satisfied with the appearance by wiping away the protective varnish that may have bloomed on the canvas surface during its trans-Atlantic voyage. This simple bit of housekeeping seemed to have done the trick as a satisfied Lenox quickly purchased a more recent 1845 effort by Turner, Fort Vimieux that features a fiery red sunset to which a muted sky appears to be totally immune. The newly minted Turner fan then made an offer to buy The Fighting Temeraire for a jaw-dropping sum of almost 10,000 American dollars – this at a time when a good working wage was one dollar a day. Turner politely refused the offer.

Such an investment in J.M.W. Turner could be problematic. His cavalier attitude towards quality materials was attributed to a parsimonious nature, but the artist tended to choose materials that looked good when applied to the canvas; posterity was not something that rested heavily on Turner's shoulders. He especially favored carmine at his easel, a pigment made from crushed insect casings that he knew was not long-lasting. Turner's watercolors were especially worrisome. In later years, museums would have to assure trustees that Turner's watercolors were not fading; in fact, they were stored in complete darkness, and when exhibited were kept in glass cases shielded by blinds.

While James Lenox was building one of the first American art collections, there had never been an integrated school of art in the United States. The first such movement was gathering momentum, however, and Joseph Mallord William Turner was an important part of its inspiration. It was called the Hudson River School, and featured a loose coalition of landscape painters who sought to capture the majesty of the American wilderness on canvas.

At its head was Thomas Cole. Cole, an English emigrant is generally given the credit as founder of the Hudson River School, not that he coined the phrase but because he settled in the Hudson River Valley in the 1820s and began painting evocative landscapes and Romantic allegorical interpretations. His early success enabled him to take a Grand Tour of Europe, studying the Old Masters and popular practitioners such as Turner and John Constable.

Like Turner, Cole began placing people in the foreground of his paintings to contrast humankind's insignificance in the glory of nature. Like Turner the artists of the Hudson River School experimented with atmospheric lighting and the play of the light source on the water and sky. Cole died in 1848 at the age of 47 when he contracted pleurisy. His friend Asher Brown Durand, mostly a currency engraver in the early days of his career, picked up the baton for the second generation of Hudson River School painters as their influence spread to the expanding frontier that was constantly expanding in the mid-19th century.

While it is easy to see the influence of Turner's colors and lights on the Hudson River School, his impact was even more far-reaching on the Impressionist Movement. Technically, the brushed colors of the scene were more critical to impressionists in the composition than definitive lines and contours, a page torn directly from Turner's playbook. It was the impression of the object, often discerned through reflected light, that created the landscape. The line from Turner to the Impressionists was so taut that some 20th century scholars would mis-identify him as an Impressionist in spite of his pre-dating the movement by decades.

By the middle of his career, and certainly in his work during the 1840s Turner was throwing away the conventions of figurative description. Édouard Manet and Claude Monet would abandon realism altogether while promoting their signature brands of impressionism. Turner was an exception in the way he worked in his early landscapes, making sketches in nature while most painters were cooped up in studios executing still lifes and portraits. When the Impressionists went outside to capture the ethereal effects of sunlight as Turner had before them, they even coined a word for the technique - "en plein air."

In 1847, the Venetian canalscape *Venice from the Steps of the Europa* became the first of Turner's works to hang in the National Gallery, a rare tribute to a living artist. The National Gallery was started in 1824 to tell the story of Western European painting pushing back to the 13th century. The collection began when the British government bought 38 paintings from the collection of John Julius Angerstein, a banker. In 1838, the National Gallery moved onto Trafalgar Square where it remains today.

Turner had complained of flagging health as early as 1841, and suffered a serious illness in 1842. He made his last visit to continental Europe in 1843, and began work on a new series of marine paintings he called *Whalers*. Turner was able to send a few canvasses to the Royal Academy - which he could address to himself as he put in a stint as acting president - for display, but the productive period of his career was over in his 70th year in 1845.

Chapter 7: Death and Legacy

Following the death of his father in late 1829, J.M.W. Turner became even more reclusive than his normally secretive self. He began spending more and more time in the seaside town of his youth, Margate, where he took lodgings with the twice-widowed Sophia Caroline Booth. Her first husband had perished at sea, and her second husband died in 1833.

The two eventually became companions and the acclaimed maritime painter answered to the name "Admiral Booth" while in her company, or sometimes it was Puggy Booth. In 1846, Turner brought Mrs. Booth and a son from her first husband to London to a house overlooking the Thames in Chelsea. He left his quarters on Queen Anne Street in the hands of the doddering spinster Hannah Danby, now ill and decrepit herself. The property would quickly run down as she lived out her years among herds of Manx cats - a canvas of Turner's, *Fishing upon the Blythe-Sand*, served as a pet door for the cats going in and out of the house.

Turner was not in much better shape. He was rarely seen in public anymore, and gave little regard for his appearance. He would have London cabs leave him off many blocks from his expansive residence at 6 Davis Place so as not to reveal his identity - not that having the shabbily dressed Turner in front of the elegant townhouse would likely be giving away the information that the mysterious Admiral Booth was the actual master of the residence.

Turner surrendered his role as Deputy President of the Royal Academy Council after 22 years on the ruling body. In 1847, the only painting he exhibited in the Academy was a repainted canvas from half-a-century earlier. The next year would be the first since 1824 when no Turners would be exhibited at all in the Royal Academy.

About this time, Turner, ever open to new technology, became interested in photography, the first daguerreotypes having been introduced in 1839 by French artist and chemist Louis Daguerre. In England, Turner befriended John Jabez Edwin Mayall who helped run his family dye works in Yorkshire before throwing himself into the infant art of "Photography" in both America and England. Mayall always considered himself and artist and not a photographer, although he clearly was not wired into the London art scene.

Turner began visiting Mayall's studio in 1847, and was a regular caller for two years, but only late in their acquaintance did Mayall come to realize who the curious septuagenarian was who had been haunting his studio for the better part of two years. Naturally, England's finest atmospheric landscape painter was entranced by the light effects that appeared on the images that formed on the highly polished silver surfaces. Mayall's daguerreotypes of Niagara Falls were especially fascinating to Turner as the two tossed ideas of shadow and light back and forth. Eventually Mayall executed "several admirable daguerreotype portraits" of the elderly Turner, still not knowing his subject was Britain's finest living artist. Sadly, an assistant unwittingly erased the historic images from the plates, which Turner and Mayall were attempting to manipulate into images in the fashion of the Old Masters.

The increasingly frail Turner eventually drifted out of photography, but not before encouraging Mayall to keep at his work at a time when the younger man was despairing of ever making his way in photography, artist or not. Mayall would indeed persevere and exhibited successfully at the Great Exhibition of 1851 in the Crystal Palace in Hyde Park, and in 1860 took the first photographs of Queen Victoria.

For years, Turner had been looking for someone to help him restore large paintings that were piled up in every corner of his haphazard studio. "If I could find a young man acquainted with picture cleaning and would help me to clean accidental stains away, it would be a happiness to drag them from their dark abode," he complained to a colleague in 1844.

One day in 1848, he was in his regular Chelsea barber shop for a shave and a trim. Somehow, Turner let his true identity come out, and the barber happily confided that his younger brother had aspirations to be a painter. Caught in a rare moment of bonhomie Turner agreed to see the young man's drawings. When he arrived at Turner's house, he was impressed enough with Francis Sherrell's portfolio that he took him on as an assistant in exchange for some painting lessons. Once again, Turner had a studio assistant by way of a barber shop.

In the autumn of 1848, England was in the grips of a cholera epidemic with hundreds of people dying across the country every day. Turner was mortified of the disease, dating to a widespread outbreak back in 1831. Lists of the numbers of dead were published in the daily papers, and advice to avoid the plague was passed around, but it was not then known that cholera was a water-borne disease. Despite his terrified efforts, Turner caught the disease. Oddly, if he had not moved to the "fresh air" of Chelsea, where flooding was common, but stayed at 47 Queen Anne Street even in its dilapidated state, where the streets were paved and drainage good, he likely would have avoided his fate. As it was, a weakened Turner survived the bout with cholera.

As Turner's health deteriorated, his teeth began to cause him no end of pain, and he had them all removed. Unable to bite, his doctor put him on a diet of rum and milk and he sucked on meat for sustenance with raw gums. Still, he rallied and reworked an 1810 canvas, *Wreck of a Transport Ship*, for exhibition at the British Institution. In 1850, he produced four pictures for the Royal Academy, the last exhibition he would have after more than 50 years as a member. The last works were well-received, betraying no halting brushstrokes that may have been expected from a master fading away.

After May 1850, it would be another 18 months before the lights went out permanently. During that time, his bent-over, crumpled figure was still seen from time to time at the Royal Academy, but by this time he was under the near-constant care of doctors. The end came on the morning of December 19, at 10:00, with the sunlight shining through the window and filling the room.

Turner had left 1000 pounds for a funeral and other assorted post-mortem expenses. His body was moved to his gallery of nearly a half-century standing on Queen Anne Street to lie in state. His friend George Jones created a solemn canvas of the occasion, set among Turner's impressive gallery pictures. In accordance to his stated desire to "be buried among my Brothers in Art" Turner was interred at St. Paul's Cathedral, in a crypt near his first booster at the Royal Academy of Arts, Joshua Reynolds, and his great champion, Thomas Lawrence.

The London Times spilled ink replaying his long career in its obituary and did not omit the criticism of Turner from his earliest watercolors. But in the end, the British newspaper of record conceded that most of the art community "admitted to his superiority in poetry, feeling, fancy and genius', and treated him with 'that reverential respect and estimation which is given to other artists by posterity alone."

Joseph Mallord William Turner sat down to draw up his first will late in 1829 after his father had died. He directed his paintings toward the nation of England and the then newly-formed National Gallery. The early paintings in the National Gallery collection were works from the Italian, Dutch and Flemish schools and were contained in a three-story townhouse called Pall Mall. The Gallery operated with no formal collection policy and despite its grand mission to display the history of Western art the paintings assembled were reflections only of the personal whims of the Trustees.

It was observing this random collection that gave Turner his ideas for where he wanted his paintings to be displayed in the nascent assemblage. He directed two of his paintings to hang with two works by Claude. Specifically, he requested *Dido building Carthage* and *Sun Rising through Vapour* to hang with *Seaport with Embarkation of the Queen of Sheba* and *The Mill*. But his demise was still more than two decades in the future at that time. In 1848, Turner had another go at his will, and this time he bequeathed all his finished paintings to the National Gallery and stipulated that they be gathered in a single room in the museum's new, more spacious quarters on Trafalgar Square.

After Turned died, the extent of Turner's fortune that had been accumulated mostly in the shadows, especially in his later years, became known. There was approximately 140,000 pounds, and most of it was earmarked for a charity to assist "decayed artists." The revelation of that sum of money and its dubious destination brought relatives, very distant relatives of the unmarried only adult child, streaming in from around England. Their cause was promoted by Jabez Tepper, a cousin several times removed.

Tepper, a solicitor, acted as the mouthpiece for all his kin. He put before the court that such a noble philanthropic gesture was illegal. It took until 1856 but the courts finally agreed with Tepper and awarded all of Turner's finished pictures and artistic works to the nation of England and the rest of the Turner estate - meaning money - to "relatives." While the National Gallery wrestled with how to display the more than 1000 oil paintings and watercolors, 30,000 drawings and 300 sketchbooks now in its possession, Tepper and his family would go on squabbling in court among themselves over their financial windfall for several more years.

Through the 1850s, only the two Turners hanging with the Claudes were displayed in the National Gallery. The rest were herded into the Marlborough House in Pall Mall and after the Prince of Wales set up house in that building in 1859, the Turner pictures were shuffled further away to the South Kensington Museum. Finally, in 1861, the "Turner Collection" began returning to the National Gallery, and finally, in 1876, the paintings were displayed as the artist had requested.

The critic John Ruskin had been one of eight executors of Turner's will, and the job fell to him to make sense of the massive trove of Turner's work after his death. Ruskin had been expected to write the biography of Joseph Mallord William Turner, but instead he spent much of the end of 1857 and the first part of 1858 wrestling with his hero's unfinished paintings and thousands of drawings.

Ruskin did manage to bring order to the Turner Bequest but along the way he discovered the man whose talent he considered heaven-sent also possessed very earthly desires. He came across the carefully bound sketchbooks of eroticism which an unamused Ruskin considered downright pornographic. He justified their existence by attributing the "rubbish" to a creeping mental illness in Turner. In December of 1858, Ruskin made certain that his "disgusting discovery" was burned in his presence, depriving the art world a chance to experience a complete appraisal of all of J.M.W. Turner's work.

The first biography of Turner was produced by George Walter Thornbury, the son of a solicitor who was trained as a journalist, and wrote fiction, history and art criticism as well. *The Life of J. M. W. Turner, R.A.* was published in 1862 when Thornbury was 34 years old. The author used Turner's original letters and papers and Ruskin was ever-present in the process. Thornbury described the experience with the critic as being akin to be "very much like working bareheaded under a tropical sun!" He would die when he was only 48 years old, inside the Camberwell House Asylum, said to have been felled by overwork.

The first memorial of Turner appeared the same year as his initial biography. Patrick McDowell, an Irish sculptor then in his sixties, executed the marble statue that was placed in the nave at St. Paul's Cathedral. McDowell created an imposing caricature while also portraying his subject's awkwardness. McDowell had been exhibiting at the Royal Academy since 1822; he had been recommended for the school by John Constable, the noted and vocal rival of Turner who dismissed the Cockney artist as "uncouth."

In 1897, the National Gallery carved out a special museum for the National Gallery of British Art - which was the original idea of Sir John Leicester, Baron de Tabley in founding the museum seventy years prior, before its scope of interest expanded to include all of Europe. The collection building rose on the site of Millbank Prison, once London's largest penitentiary that was demolished beginning in 1892.

Most of the Turner collection arrived in the new museum in 1910. Henry Tate, who made his fortune selling sugar cubes, was the major donor for the new gallery and also gave his private collection to help it along, resulting in his name appearing on the marquee. Save for an adventure during World War II, when the entire national collection was spirited to Wales for safe storage in castles during German bombing raids, the Turners have been part of the Tate Museum ever since.

In 1984, the museum initiated the Turner Prize, a recognition for British visual artists under the age of 50 that immediately became the country's most talked-about art award. The Turner Prize boasts a bit of everything that would make its namesake proud. The competing artists troll in innovative media such as installation art, non-traditional sculpture and video art, which would have no doubt fascinated a modern-facing J.M.W. Turner. The Turner Prize also comes with a healthy cash prize, juiced by commercial sponsorship, all of which the master artist would no doubt endorse. Most of all, Turner would revel in the entries for the prize named for him that have sparked controversy from its earliest entries. The artist, whose volumes of erotic drawings were destroyed and explained away as being caused by brain sickness, would have marveled at the reception of Death, an action sculpture that showed cheap plastic blow-up sex dolls enjoying each other and sex toys on an inflatable pool mattress. In fact, it was a bronze sculpture painted to look plastic.

Entries like this have been credited with bringing young people into galleries and generating buzz about British art. Just as vocal are the critics of the Turner Prize, a trope with which the artist was all too familiar. At the first artist demonstration against the Turner Prize, disgruntled artists accused the competition of deteriorating into an "ongoing national joke" and claiming, "the only artist who wouldn't be in danger of winning the Turner Prize is Turner." The year was 2000, but the words might not have been out of place 200 years earlier in the halls of the Royal Academy at a Turner exhibition.

Meanwhile, the discussion of Turner's merit as an artist that dogged him in some fashion throughout his career has quieted. When the National Gallery collection was re-assembled after World War II, the museum chose to break the terms of the Turner Bequest to which it adhered for most of a century. The two Turners were no longer displayed with the two Claudes, and the decision was explained thusly: "The moral issue raised by the terms of Turner's will is no longer in question given that Turner's reputation as Claude's equal was now acknowledged, and it would scarcely be necessary for that reason alone to continue the arrangement."

In the 21st century, with the 250th anniversary of his birth on the not-too-distant horizon Joseph Mallord William Turner has been on a roll. In addition to his expansive legacy in the Tate, the Turner Contemporary Gallery was built in the seaside town of Margate which played a critical role in Turner's life at various times for six decades. The broad mission of the gallery interprets British and international art from Turner and his influences to the present. The post-modern building overlooks the harbor on land where Turner once lived in a boarding house. Pictures that were on loan from around the world were gathered for a major retrospective entitled "Turner's Britain" in 2003 at the Birmingham Museum and Art Gallery. Included in the exhibition was *The Fighting Téméraire* that got the nod as Britain's favorite painting the following year.

In October 2007, over 140 Turners - about evenly divided between oils and works on paper - were assembled for the largest and most comprehensive exhibition of the landscape painter's vision ever put on in the United States. There were stops at the National Gallery in Washington, the Metropolitan Museum of Art in New York City and the Dallas Museum of Art. A team of American curators worked with the Tate Museum to bring such significant works as Snow Storm: Hannibal and His Army Crossing the Alps and his sole Royal Commission, The Battle of Trafalgar, 21 October 1805 out of England for the first time.

And the insurance could not have been cheap. A year earlier, Christie's had put up for auction *Giudecca, La Donna Della Salute and San Giorgio*, from Turner's later period, 1841. It was one of his Venetian series that had so rankled critics at the time, a dream-like vision of gondola boats being poled past The Doge's Palace on a characteristically shrouded Giudecca Canal. After being exhibited in the Royal Academy four times, the painting had most recently been on display in the Art Institute of Chicago, on loan from the St. Francis of Assisi Foundation, who had been given the picture by an unknown European collector.

Christie's put an estimate of $15 million on the dreamy Venetian canal scene, but when the gavel came down the winning bid was $35.8 million, a record for a Turner painting. The winning bidder was as mysterious as the benefactor of the Capuchin priests, having sent his bids in over the telephone. It turned out to be casino magnate Steve Wynn, perhaps spurred on by expert evaluations that stated: "You can truly label this a masterpiece. It's something to do with the transparency of the water and the way the buildings in the background seem to dissolve in the light. It's suggestive of impressionism but at the same time it remains a clearly realistic view of Venice. The condition of the painting is flawless. It's as fresh as the day it was painted - you can see every individual brushstroke."

Wynn's acquisition was about three times the previous record for a Turner when some $13 million pried *Seascape, Folkestone* out of the collection of broadcaster and art historian Lord Kenneth Clark in 1984. But Wynn was bidding in a bull market for Turners. His *Heidelberg with a Rainbow*, another creation from Turner's last burst of productivity in the 1840s, had recently sold for more money than any other British watercolor when it fetched more than £2 million at auction, about three times what was anticipated.

Giudecca, La Donna Della Salute and San Giorgio was destined to become just a footnote in Turner's catalog as well. In 2010, its record auction price was surpassed when the J. Paul Getty Museum in Los Angeles picked up *Modern Rome - Campo Vaccino* for a check of $44.9 million. Once again, the winning bid on a Turner at auction was about three times what was anticipated. Modern Rome - Campo Vaccino brought the curtain down on Turner's more than two decades of exploring the Italian capital on canvas. Completed in 1839, his last picture of Rome was fittingly a vision of ruins of the Roman Forum shimmering against the haze of the city. After being exhibited in the Royal Academy, the painting was acquired by Turner's close friend and occasional traveling companion, Hugh Andrew Johnstone Munro of Novar.

It was bought out of the unmarried Munro's estate in 1878 by Archibald Primrose, 5th Earl of Rosebery, who would spend 15 months as British Prime Minister in the 1890s. Modern Rome - Campo Vaccino hung in the family residence at Mentmore in Buckinghamshire for over a century before doing a stint in the National Gallery. Sotheby's called Modern Rome "undoubtedly among the most important of Turner's works ever to come to auction." It now hangs in the United States, waiting until the next immaculately conditioned Turner comes on the market to beat its record.

Joseph Mallord William Turner has certainly been validated by the art world as one of Britain's greatest, if not absolute greatest painter. In 2014, he received the ultimate stamp of cultural approval: a Hollywood biopic. Mike Leigh, who has spent a career depicting the British ethos on stage and screen, debuted *Mr. Turner* at the Cannes Film Festival in France.

The movie depicts the final decades of J.M.W. Turner's life as the landscape painter was both reviled and revered by the art world and the public. You get a sense of Turner's position in English society while living stealthily in Chelsea. You get his travels to aristocratic country homes, foreign lands and brothels. You even get Turner strapped to a ship's mast in a snow storm to paint *Snow Storm — Steam-Boat off a Harbour's Mouth making Signals in Shallow Water*. And the film does not shy away from Turner's carnal hijinks. English character actor Timothy Spall walked away from Cannes with a Best Actor award for his portrayal of the enigmatic artist that John Ruskin once called ""the only perfect landscape painter."

Bibliography

BBC News; "Turner wins 'great painting' vote," September 5, 2005.

Bennett, Will, The Telegraph; Turner that failed to set sail," January 29, 2002.

Chignell, Robert; J.M.W. Turner, R.A., Minneapolis: The Walter Scott Publishing Company, 1902.

Honigsbaum, Mark, The Guardian; "Turner's hidden masterpiece likely to fetch British sale record," November 21, 2005.

Leight, Michele, City Review; "Ruskin, Turner and the Pre-Raphaelites," 2000.

London Daily News; "Colors That Fade - Turner's Masterpieces; Can His Works Be Saved?", January 9, 1930.

Monkhouse, William Cosmo; Dictionary of National Biography, 1885-1900, Volume 57, London: Oxford University Press, 1901.

Rennell, Tony, London Daily Mail; "Sex, feuds, money: What Britain's greatest ever painter JMW Turner REALLY prized," September 25, 2009.

Thornbury, George Walter; The Life of J.M.W. Turner, London: Hurst and Blackett, Publishers, 1862.

Vogel, Carol, The New York Times; "Who Paid $35.8 Million for J. M. W. Turner's View of Venice?", April 8, 2006.

Whittingham, Selby, The Quarterly Review; "Turner – visionary or conservative?," 2013.

Wilton, Andrew; Turner in His Time, London: Thames & Hudson, 2007.

Printed in Great Britain
by Amazon.co.uk, Ltd.,
Marston Gate.